Auld Lang Syne
A Portrait of Robert Burns

by Elisabeth Fraser

To Dr Moore, Burns wrote:
'It ever was my opinion that the mistakes and blunders both in a rational and religious point of view, of which we see thousands daily guilty are owing to their ignorance of themselves. To know myself has been all along my constant study. I weighed myself alone; I balanced myself with others; I watched every means of information, to see how much ground I occupied as a man and as a poet; I studied assiduously Nature's design in my formation – where the lights and shades in my character were intended.'

Jarrold Colour Publications, Norwich.

Burns and the Vision. Painting by James Christie, by
courtesy of the Irvine Burns Club

Burns was apparently musing by the fireplace one
evening in the parlour of the farmhouse at Mossgiel,
when the 'reek' (smoke) curled in front of him to form
this strange vision.

Contents

Auld Lang Syne

Introduction

Information about the great Scottish poet, Robert Burns, has been gathered over the years, since his death in 1796; all of it has contributed to portray the life and work of this remarkable man. Above all his letters, in themselves, have assisted scholars to not only understand his poetical works, but they have also formed an important insight into his life and character. The Burns family have submitted letters, documents and possessions relating to the poet. Volumes have been written about him. There are records with regard to his military service with the Royal Dumfries Volunteers, his Masonic Lodge connections and his occupation as an Excise Officer in and around Dumfries. Great works of art have portrayed him in various aspects of his life. The Burns Federation plays an important part in keeping his memory alive and linking together the many Burns clubs now formed all over the world.

The following synopsis on Burns life, together with the Burns Country map will help the reader to follow his activities. The songs and poems selected in this book are among Burns' most popular. We hope that the reader will be inspired to make a closer contact with the many places related to this unique Scottish Bard, and to gain a deeper insight into his works.

Scotland's Farmer Poet

Robert Burns, one of the greatest, some feel *the* greatest, Scottish poets of the eighteenth century had and still has a profound influence upon the literary world. He was undoubtedly a genius, with a remarkable talent for portraying the truth of what he saw in daily life. His 'innocent' mind enabled him to capture in words the exact truth, without any thought of the consequence.

The poet was born on 25 January 1759, in Alloway near Ayr. When his father was riding to fetch a doctor to assist at Robert's birth, he helped an old gypsy woman to cross a flooded stream. In gratitude, she visited the new-born baby, gave him her blessing and predicted his fame. The cottage of his birth is now world famous. It is under the care of The Trustees of Burns Cottage and Monument. In 1898 The Trustees built a separate Museum close by the cottage to house priceless paintings, manuscripts and other documents and objects associated with the poet and his family. Other rooms have since been added as the collection increased.

Left: *Portrait of Burns at Lady Stairs, Edinburgh.* Painting by C. M. Hardie; by courtesy of the City of Edinburgh District Council
Below: *Burns Cottage.* Watercolour by Hugh William Williams; by courtesy of the National Galleries of Scotland, Edinburgh.

Souter Johnnie's cottage with the statue characters from *Tam o' Shanter*; by courtesy of the National Trust for Scotland

Burns Suppers are celebrated in many parts of the world to commemorate the birth of this great poet. Nowhere more so than Scotland. These famous suppers originated in Greenock some five years after Burns' death. His famous song 'Auld Lang Syne' which is always sung at these suppers is unique, with a penetrating quality of bringing people together wherever they may be.

The Land O' Burns Centre at Alloway has an excellent audio-visual on the Burns Heritage Trail, produced by the Kyle and Carrick District Council to honour the life of Burns. (See the map on pages 18–19.)

It is hard to imagine today what the eighteenth century held for such a genius. There was little or no mass media or public relations to aid such talent. Burns had to rely upon friends and acquaintances for their introductions to learned men. With very little money and only a farming background, this was by no means easy. Yet, Burns *did* gain, during his lifetime a very favourable reputation both for his verse and his songs, and he *was* received by the highest society of the day.

When Burns was six years old his father, William Burnes, engaged a young teacher, John Murdoch, to set up a small school in Alloway. The school was organised to take some local children in addition to the Burnes' family. John Murdoch, who became the lifelong friend of the poet, received from Burns the highest tribute a schoolmaster could wish from his pupil. 'I have not forgotten, nor will I ever forget, the many obligations I lie under to your kindness and friendship.' When Burns was not in the schoolroom, he was helping his father on their farm and eventually became the principal labourer, for William Burnes employed no hired hands. The poet wrote of this period: 'The cheerless gloom of a hermit, with the unceasing moil of a galley-slave, brought me to my sixteenth year, a little before which I committed the sin of rhyme.' In his eighteenth year Burns spent the summer at Kirkoswald learning higher mathematics and surveying at Hugh Rodger's School. But during this period of his life Burns felt he had made more progress in the understanding of mankind, than he ever had from his lessons. It is interesting to note that at Kirkoswald in the restored ale-house in the garden of Souter Johnnie's cottage there are life-size sculptures of the characters portrayed in Burns' famous poem *Tam o' Shanter*. This cottage is under the care of the National Trust for Scotland.

It was in 1780 that a few of the young men of Tarbolton, formed themselves into a literary and debating society with Burns as their President. The building where they held their meetings was called the Bachelors' Club and is now under the care of the National Trust for Scotland. In the

The Bachelors' Club, Tarbolton

following year the poet was admitted as an apprentice to St David's Tarbolton Lodge of Freemasons; becoming Deputy Grand Master of the Lodge in 1784. Towards the end of 1781 Burns entered into a partnership with his uncle, Alexander Peacock, a flax-dresser in Irvine. This enterprise proved disastrous, the poet was swindled by his uncle and the shop was burnt down during the New Year Carousal in 1782. Today, the Heckling Shop as it was called, has been restored to as near the original state as possible – including the thatched roof – by the Irvine Development Corporation and other interested parties. The shop is within the Glasgow Vennel and is linked with a Studio Gallery Museum and the Ayrshire Writers and Artists Society. The Glasgow Vennel is a cobbled street rich in history, now looking as it was in Burns' day. Not far from here is 'Wellwood', the Irvine Burns Club, with a very fine museum and library, one of the oldest continuous Burns clubs in the world. One of the rare first editions of Burns' poems, printed in Kilmarnock together with many of its rare original manuscripts, form part of the invaluable collection. C. M. Hardie's *Burns in Edinburgh*, an oil painting, showing Burns with the Duchess of Gordon is one of their most prized works of art (pages 10–11).

The Heckling Shop, Glasgow Vennel

The disappointment at Irvine, coupled with his father's illness put Burns into a deep state of depression. He returned to Lochlea to help his father with the farm. Unfortunately, not long after his return his father died. Much affected by this Burns wrote of his father 'the tender father, and generous friend now at rest from the many buffetings of an evil world, against which he so long and so bravely struggled'. (See page 36 'My Father was a Farmer'.)

In 1784 Gilbert, his brother, and Robert subleased a farm at Mossgiel, near Mauchline. The farm was of some 118 acres, and every member of the family who laboured on the farm received a wage. It was at Mauchline that Burns came into contact with men of a position somewhat better than his own. He was now twenty-five years old, with a great love of life; his clever wit, and natural muse made him welcome wherever he went.

The installation of Burns as Poet Laureate of the lodge, Canongate, Kilwinning. Painting by Stewart Watson; by courtesy of the National Galleries of Scotland, Edinburgh

It was during the year of 1785 that Burns first met Jean Armour. The story of the romance began through a chance remark made by the poet about his beloved dog. He was heard to say that if he could find a lass as faithful as his dog he would marry her. One day, Jean Armour was hanging out some washing as Burns was passing by her home; she coyly called to the poet, enquiring if he had found the lass of his dreams. Burns fell deeply in love with Jean. This romantic love affair was destined to bring great anguish and concern to Burns. For when Jean's father heard that his daughter was expecting a baby, he forbade the marriage, refusing to accept Burns' written acknowledgment which, according to Scottish Law, would have been accepted as evidence of an irregular marriage. Jean was sent to Paisley to friends of the family. This so affected the poet, that he made plans to emigrate. He had been offered a job in Jamaica at thirty pounds per year – but it was not to be. Plans were well advanced when Burns wrote: 'I had taken farewell of my friends and my chest was on the road to Greenock when I had composed a song "The gloomy night is gathering fast" which was to be my last effort of my muse in Caledonia, when a letter from Mr Blacklock, the blind Poet, to a friend of mine, overthrew all my schemes by arousing my poetic ambitions.'

This change of heart spurred Burns to give to the world a brilliant series of poems, and in 1786 Burns' first edition of poems and songs was published by John Wilson of Kilmarnock, price three shillings. Before the first edition was printed, the family agreed to change their surname from Burnes to Burns. When the poet sought to reprint he could not raise the twenty seven pounds needed to cover the cost of the paper. His first edition had brought him a profit of only twenty pounds. Encouraged by Dr Blacklock's praise and his many introductions, Burns set out on horseback for Edinburgh. Dr Dalrymple of Orangefield gave the poet an introduction to the Earl of Glencairn, which brought Burns into the centre of the high society of Edinburgh.

Burns never forgot the Earl of Glencairn – his generous patron – and immortalised his name in a beautiful little poem, mourning his death in 1791.

> The Bridegroom may forget the Bride
> Was made his wedded wife yestreen,
> The monarch may forget the crown
> That on his head an hour has been.
> The mother may forget her child
> That smiles so sweetly on her knee;
> But I'll remember thee, Glencairn
> And all that thou hast done for me;
> For all I have and all I am I owe to thee.

These lines appear below the memorial tablet in Falmouth Parish Church to the memory of James Cunningham, 14th Earl of Glencairn. Burns followed the poem with a touching little prayer in French, 'Oublie moi, Grand Dieu, si Jamais je l'oublie.' (Forget me O God, if I forget him.) A snuff mull presented by the Earl of Glencairn to Robert Burns is on display in Burns House, Dumfries, a prized possession of the Dumfries Burns Club.

It must have been about this time that Burns formed an attachment with Mary Campbell, though it was not until many years later that her surname was known. The bible given to her by Burns is preserved in the monument to Burns at Alloway by the Banks o' Doon; and the painting by W. H. Midwood on the front cover of this book shows Burns presenting it to Mary. The original of this painting hangs in the Burns Cottage Museum, Alloway.

One of the chief pleasures Burns derived from his visits to Edinburgh, were his early-morning walks taken in many parts of the outskirts of the city. In the early spring he often climbed to the

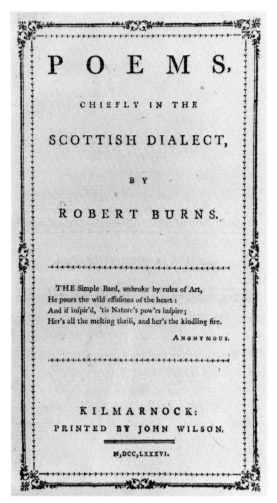

THE Simple Bard, unbroke by rules of Art,
He pours the wild effusions of the heart:
And if inspir'd, 'tis Nature's pow'rs inspire;
Her's all the melting thrill, and her's the kindling fire.

The Kilmarnock edition of *Burns' Poems*. Published 1786. By courtesy of the Irvine Burns Club

top of Arthur's Seat, surveying the silent sun rising in the clear fresh air. His chosen companion on these morning walks was his artist friend Alexander Nasmyth, also an ardent lover of nature. Burns is known to have stayed in various parts of Edinburgh: plaques over doorways and arches of inns and taverns bear his name today. While in Edinburgh he was invited to attend many poetical gatherings in the noble households of the day: in particular, by the Duchess of Gordon, who was the fashionable leader of society in Edinburgh; she was heard to say of Burns: 'That no man's conversation ever carried her so completely off her feet'. Mrs Alison Cockburn, another high society lady, wrote to a friend: 'The Town is at present agog with the Ploughman Poet, who receives adulation with native dignity, and is the very figure of his profession – strong, but coarse, yet he has a most enthusiastic heart of love.'

By far the most interesting reminiscences on Burns was made by Sir Walter Scott – then a young boy of about fifteen years, who met Burns at the home of the distinguished poet, Professor Ferguson. 'We youngsters sat silent, looked and listened,' says Scott; Burns was deeply affected by a picture of a soldier lying dead in the snow, his wife and child on one side and his dog on the other. Beneath the picture some verses were written. Burns enquired who was the poet. 'It chanced,' says Scott, 'that nobody but myself remembered that they occur in a half-forgotten poem by Langhorne's, called by the unpromising title of "The Justice of the Peace". I whispered my information to a friend present, who mentioned it to Burns, who rewarded me with a look and a word, which though of mere civility, I then received, and still recollect with very much pleasure. His person was strong and robust; his manners rustic, not clownish, a sort of dignified plainness and simplicity, which received part of its effects perhaps, from one's knowledge of his extraordinary talent. His features are represented in Mr. Nasmyth's picture, but to me it conveys the idea that they are diminished, as if in perspective. I think his countenance was more massive than it looks in any of the portraits. I would have taken the Poet, had I not known what he was, for a very sagacious country farmer of the Old Scottish School; ie. none of your modern agriculturists, who keep labourers for their drudgery, but the duced gudeman who held his own plough. There was a strong expression of sense and shrewdness in all his lineaments: his eye alone, I think, indicated the poetical character and temperament. It was large and of a dark cast which glowed, I say literally glowed, when he spoke with feeling or interest. I never saw such another eye in a human head, though I have seen the most distinguished men of my time. His conversation expressed perfect confidence, without the slightest presumption. Among the men who were the most learned of their time and country, he expressed himself with perfect firmness, but without the least intrusive forwardness. When he differed in opinion, he did not hesitate to express it firmly, yet at the same time with modesty.' Scott continues: 'He was like a farmer dressed in his best to dine with the Laird. I do not speak in malen parlem, when I say, I never saw a man when in the company with his superiors in station and information more perfectly free from either the reality or the affectation of embarrassment.'

The meeting of Sir Walter Scott and Burns at Sciences House, Edinburgh. By courtesy of Mrs Maxwell-Scott, Abbotsford

Overleaf: *Burns in Edinburgh.*
Oil painting by C. M. Hardie; by courtesy of the Irvine Burns Club

Silhouette of Clarinda (Nancy McLehose) by courtesy of the National Galleries of Scotland, Edinburgh

a greater height of song writing: nor did he lose this new-found inspiration when he returned to Dumfriesshire, where he settled for the remaining years of his life.

In September 1787 Burns and Nicol set off on their Highland tour for Inverness via Stirling and Dunkeld, returning by way of Aberdeen. In his letter to his brother Gilbert on 17 September 1787, Burns reveals that he passed through Crieff on his way to Kenmore and Aberfeldy. He stayed two nights at Blair Castle in Perthshire, the home of the Duke and Duchess of Atholl. It was at Dunkeld that he met the famous fiddler, Neil Gow. It is certain that he had a great influence on Burns' song writing, for it is known that he played many a reel for the poet. Incidentally, Burns also played the fiddle, which must have been a considerable advantage when writing his songs. He continued his journey 'in those enchanting days', visiting Sir James Grant of Grant Castle in Strathspey, calling at Cawdor Castle, the ancient seat of the Macbeths, on his way to Fort George and Inverness. On his route to Aberdeen the poet stayed overnight with Brodie of Brodie in that famous castle, dining the following day with the Duke and Duchess of Gordon at their castle at Fochabers; continuing to Aberdeen via Montrose where he called on some of his relations.

Neil Gow – the Dunkeld Fiddler by Sir Henry Raeburn. By courtesy of the National Galleries of Scotland, Edinburgh

Burns gained many friends during his lifetime, but none dearer to him than Clarinda, Mrs Nancy McLehose, whom he met in Edinburgh. He admired her capabilities very much, not only was she a poetess, but also a promising artist, so they had much in common. Her fascinating charm completely captured the poet's imagination. She was a lady of rank and position, who recognised the poet's incredible talent and encouraged him accordingly. There is little doubt that the greatest love song ever written was addressed to Clarinda in Burns' poem 'Ae Fond Kiss'.

Prior to his meeting with Clarinda the second edition of his poems was published by William Creech of Edinburgh in 1787. Much later, when Burns finally settled with Creech, he was obliged to sell his copyright for 100 guineas. He received a further £400, £180 of which he gave to his brother Gilbert for the support of their mother.

In spite of the excitement of town life, Burns never forgot Jean Armour, the whole episode had deeply affected him. It is known that Burns saw Jean many times during this period, and he often sought to resolve her father's objections to him, but with little or no success.

During one of Burns' visits to Edinburgh a close friend, William Nicol, a school teacher, invited the poet to join him in a tour of the Highlands of Scotland. The rugged mountains with their majestic scenery, together with the wildness of the country life, inspired the poet to

Marble statue of Burns by J. Flaxman; by courtesy of the National Galleries of Scotland, Edinburgh and the City of Edinburgh District Council

John Flaxman died before the completion of the statue. However, his pupil and brother-in-law, Joseph Denman agreed to finish his work. A monument was later erected to house the statue and was placed in Regent Road, Edinburgh. Owing to the fear of deterioration and the fact that it was not easily accessible to the general public, it was decided to remove the statue to the Scottish National Portrait Gallery in Queens Street, Edinburgh where it is on display today. This very fine statue and monument are under the care of the City of Edinburgh and District Council.

In St Giles Cathedral, Edinburgh, there is a magnificent stained-glass window above the west door dedicated to the memory of Robert Burns. This work was designed by Leifur Breidfjord from Iceland, who trained at the

Design drawing of the Burns Memorial Window in St Giles Cathedral by Leifur Breidfjord. By courtesy of Bernard Fielden, Simpson & Brown, architects to the Cathedral

On 29 November 1788 Burns made his last visit to Edinburgh, staying about a week at the White Hart Inn in the Grassmarket. The old inn is still in the Grassmarket today, bearing the plaque above the archway for all to see that Burns stayed there.

Burns left his lasting impression of Edinburgh through his poem 'Address to Edinburgh' which he sent to his friend William Chalmers. It is not surprising that after the poet's death a statue was eventually erected in Edinburgh to honour his memory, but it was surprising that the idea originated in Bombay, through a Mr John Forbes Hamilton. A meeting, arranged by him with some of his close friends, was held in London in the Freemasons Tavern on 26 May 1821. Here it was agreed that funds amounting to about £1,500 would be available for a marble statue of Robert Burns. Thus in July 1824 an agreement was made with John Flaxman P.S.R.A., the celebrated sculptor, to commence work on a life-size statue of Burns. (The sculptor used the oil painting of Alexander Nasmyth to help him with his work.) When some doubt arose with regard to payment, the sculptor, to his credit, and because of his admiration of the Scottish bard, proposed to complete his work with or without remuneration. Unfortunately,

Ellisland Farm by J. O. Brown; by courtesy of Mrs Tom McIlwraith

Jean Armour (Mrs Burns) by J. A. Gillfillan. By courtesy of the National Galleries of Scotland, Edinburgh

Edinburgh College of Art. The stained glass symbolises love, brotherhood of man, and nature – the very essence of Burns' poetical works.

Leaving Edinburgh behind, Robert Burns began another phase of his life in Dumfriesshire. He was not able to earn enough from his muse to live independently, so when he was offered a leasing of a small farm at Ellisland he felt he could not refuse. Although the poet had an uneasy feeling that the farm was not a viable proposition, he agreed to take the lease at a much reduced rent, and the landlord gave him financial assistance to enable him to build a new farmhouse, for there was no suitable dwelling house at Ellisland. Burns wanted to settle down, and with the prospects of the farm and a new home, he again approached Jean Armour to join him at Ellisland. Their marriage took place in 1788 at Gavin Hamilton's, a Justice of the Peace, and a personal friend of the poet. Hamilton was able to provide Burns with a certificate of marriage. Indeed the certificate originally given to Jean's father was by no means void, but now the marriage was official. After a while they settled down in their new home at Ellisland.

They were a devoted family, and both parents were very fond of their children.

It was while Burns was at Ellisland that he met, through his friend and next door neighbour Robert Riddell of Friars Carse, the antiquarian, Captain Francis Grose, who was in the process of collecting material for a book he was engaged upon. Burns wanted him to include an illustration of the Old Kirk at Alloway; but the wily Captain would only agree if Burns wrote a poem around it. And so it was that Burns composed in one day the most intriguing poetical story of *Tam o' Shanter*. Jean Burns relates how she saw Burns by the riverside 'laughing and gesticulating as the humorous incidents assumed shape in the Poet's mind'.

During his years at Ellisland Burns continued to write his verse and songs, but the farm was unremunerative, so it was just as well that the poet had already applied for employment as an Excise-Officer. The farm after a time, as Burns suspected from the beginning, proved to be an ever increasing burden. He wrote to his brother Gilbert saying, 'I feel hypochondria pervading every atom of my body and soul. This farm has undone my enjoyment of myself. It is a ruinous affair on all hands.' His excise duties forced him to ride over two hundred miles a week and he was often ill in the winter months. It was not surprising that Burns finally decided to move away from the farm to Dumfries, and take up full-time employment as an Excise Officer.

It was in late 1791 that Burns eventually moved to a small house in Bank Street, Dumfries – then called The Wee Vennel. His position as an Excise Officer was an exacting one and he

Auld Kirk, Alloway, Strathclyde

became fully occupied with it. Shortly before Burns came to Dumfries, the Old Town Mill house was erected beside the River Nith. This used to grind the town's corn and now houses an Interpretation Centre, with an exhibition about Burns and his life in Dumfries. This includes a full size diorama of Burns as an Exciseman and a large scale model of Dumfries in the 1790s. There are also many original objects relating to Burns on display. This centre is under the care of the Nithdale District Council.

Eventually in 1793 Burns moved to a larger house in Mill Street, now named Burns House, Burns Street; where a most interesting museum displays many manuscripts and articles of interest associated with Burns. This is also under the care of the Nithdale District Council. It was while Burns was in Dumfries that he met George Thomson, the publisher of *Scottish Airs*. Thomson was a hard critic, but the poet had much to thank him for, indeed the very best songs written by Burns came under his scrutiny. There was much correspondence between them from 1792 to 1796, the year of the poet's death. Thomson published many of Burns' finest poems and songs during this period, including 'Auld Lang Syne'.

Burns loved researching and discovering the half-forgotten old Scottish songs and legends. He was not only able to unearth them but had the rare talent of giving them new life through the magic of his pen. Indeed, had it not been for

Burns Mausoleum, Dumfries

Burns, many of the priceless old Scottish songs would have been lost for all time. The Scots all over the world have always kept their 'home fires burning' through their songs. Burns clearly appreciated this, but his brilliant song 'Auld Lang Syne' shows the depth of his desire for the brotherhood of man and commands a universal homage. Is it not a remarkable fact, that whenever there is a festive occasion, particularly at New Year, no matter where you find yourself, those sterling words, as hands are clasped in parting, ring out their challenge to all men?

Perhaps in a way, the very fact that Burns was obliged to labour long hours during his life, had its own rewards. His closeness to nature gave him the opportunity for undisturbed observation, so when he could write his verse, he wrote what he had *seen* without embellishment. Maybe this was why his genius was so rare. The poet expressed so beautifully the smallest creature in nature, with such exactitude and grace. For example, 'To a Mouse' and 'To a Louse'. There is a lovely story that tells us how Burns came to write 'To a Mouse'. He was ploughing the fields one day with John Blane, when a mouse's nest was unearthed. John Blane attacked it with his prattle (plough spade). Burns stopped him instantly, becoming quiet and remote for the rest of the day. Later in the early hours of the morning he awoke John Blane, handing him the

Burns House, Dumfries

poem 'To a Mouse'. 'Now,' said Burns, 'what do you think of the wee mouse?'

'Holy Willie's Prayer' was another example of the poet's rare talent for expressing the truth *as it is*. This poem is said to be the 'most terrible commentary on the Calvinistic doctrine ever written'. Briefly the poem relates how Burns' friend Gavin Hamilton, a lawyer, had been refused the ordinance of the Church, because he was believed to have made a journey on the Sabbath, and because one of his servants, by his orders, had brought in some potatoes from the garden on another Sunday. Ironically, the very elder who had forced this upon Hamilton was caught taking church funds and eventually died in a ditch in a helpless state of intoxication.

In 1796 Burns' health was causing concern. He was sent to Brow Well on the Solway Coast, a miserable spa with three cottages and a large tank. The mineral spring water was fed into the tank by a pipe. In spite of being a very sick man, Burns took the waters each day, supposedly to relieve his rheumatism, he also bathed in the sea. There is a plaque at Brow Well relating to Burns' visit. The poet was unable to regain his former strength and returned home. He continually worried about the welfare of his wife and family; his wife was expecting their last child, which must have greatly added to his troubles. It is an extraordinary fact that, today, the first edition of Burns' poems would fetch a fortune, yet, in Burns' day, the poet received very little remuneration for his masterpieces. Unable to cope any longer with his ill health he was forced to his bed; he lingered only a few days. As he lay dying he is reported to have said to his wife: 'Don't be afraid. I'll be more thought of a hundred years hence, than I am at present.' He died on 21 July 1796 in his thirty-eighth year, in his home at Mill Street, Dumfries. He was buried with full military honours in St Michael's churchyard. The poet was a well-respected member of the Royal Dumfries Volunteers. Two regiments were in Dumfries at the time of his death, that of the Fencible Infantry of Angusshire and the Cinque Ports Cavalry, both were in attendance at Burns' funeral. In 1815 his remains were transferred to the elegant mausoleum erected in honour of his memory in the same churchyard.

In his short lifetime, Burns became one of the greatest Scottish poets, gaining a world-wide reputation that is both remarkable and exceptional in every way. In a strange way, too, he immortalised himself by his own song, 'Auld Lang Syne'. It would be hard to find another song with a greater appeal to highlight the festive celebrations of bringing in each New Year; or to find another poet who could touch the hearts of all men everywhere, so completely, through the magic of his verse.

Burns at an evening party at Lord Monboddo's. Wash drawing by James Edgar; by courtesy of the National Galleries of Scotland, Edinburgh

Firth of Clyde

Millport Largs

Burns Garden

Motherwell
Hamilton
East Kilbride

Eglinton Woods

Kilwinning

Burns Monument and Museum
Dean Castle

Dick Institute

Ardrossan

KILMARNOCK Newmilns

Laigh and Old High Kirks

Glasgow Vennel, Irvine

Saltcoats

Irvine

Darvel
Greenholm

STR

Brodick

Galston

Irvine Burns Club Museum

Troon

Mauchline Kirkyard

A77

A70

Castle Montgomery

Tarbolton

Mauchline

Poosie Nansie's Tavern

Prestwick

Failford

Bachelors' Club

AYR

Alloway

Holmhead
Cumnock

Burns House Museum

A76

Auld Kirk

River Nith

Auld Brig

Tam O'Shanter Museum

A719 A77

Maybole

Kirkoswald

River Doon

Highland Mary's Monument

New Cumnock

Sanquhar

Alloway Kirk

Loch Doon

Burns Memorial Tower

Afton Water

Burns Monument

Ailsa Craig

Girvan

Burns Cottage and Museum

Land o' Burns Centre

Leglen Wood

Culzean Castle and Country Park

A765

Brig o' Doon

Clatteringshaws Loch

A713

A702

Loch Ure

River Dee

A77

A714

Kirkoswald Churchyard

River Cree

Souter Johnnie's House

A712

New Galloway

A713

Ure Water

A762

Loch Ken

Cairnryan

A718

Water of Luce

Newton Stewart

B769

D U M

F R I E S

Gatehouse of Fleet

Castle Douglas

STRANRAER

A75

A75

Wigtown

A75

A75

A77

Murray Arms Hotel

Kirkudbright

A711

A716

A747

A714

A746

Selkirk Arms Hotel

Luce Bay

Whithorn

Wigtown Bay

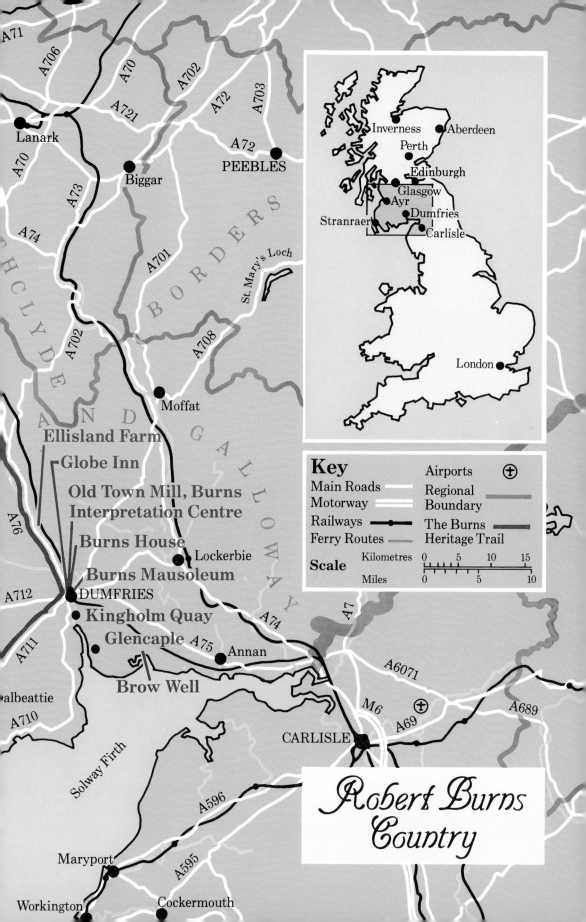

A71

A706

A70

A702

A721

A72

A703

Lanark

Biggar

A72

PEEBLES

A70

A73

A74

A701

B O R D E R S

St. Mary's Loch

A702

A708

Moffat

Ellisland Farm

A N D

G A L L O W A Y

Globe Inn

Old Town Mill, Burns
Interpretation Centre

A76

Burns House

Lockerbie

Burns Mausoleum

A712

DUMFRIES

Kingholm Quay

A711

Glencaple

A75

Annan

A74

A7

Brow Well

albeattie

A710

Solway Firth

CARLISLE

A6071

M6

A69

A689

Maryport

A596

A595

Cockermouth

Workington

Key

Main Roads

Motorway

Railways

Ferry Routes

Scale

Airports ✈

Regional
Boundary

The Burns
Heritage Trail

Kilometres

0   5   10   15

Miles

0   5   10

Inverness

Aberdeen

Perth

Edinburgh

Glasgow

Ayr

Stranraer

Dumfries

Carlisle

London

*Robert Burns
Country*

The Burns Federation

The worldwide organisation of clubs and societies, formed to do honour to and perpetuate the memory of Robert Burns, is a unique phenomenon without parallel in the literature or culture of any nation other than the Scots. All countries have their national poets, but even within the confines of their native land these men are not accorded the adulation and the widespread popular acclaim, attended by public celebrations of all kinds, which have been the tribute paid to Burns; nor are their admirers and devotees banded together in the way that Burnsians the world over have organised themselves for the past 180 years. The Burns cult defies definition or rational explanation, but it exists. Towards the end of January each year countless thousands of people in every corner of the globe meet in a convivial atmosphere to sing his songs and recite his poetry and to toast the 'Immortal Memory' of Burns, the farmer-poet from a small country on the north-western fringe of Europe, who lived and died two centuries ago, but who today is revered as the Poet of all Mankind.

Anniversary dinners were being held by his friends within a few short years of his untimely death. Within a decade, Burns Night had taken on the character of a national celebration. In 1859, when the centenary of his birth occurred, the event was celebrated all over the world. Wherever Scots migrated they preserved the distinctive elements of their culture and language, and Robert Burns became a national symbol. In more recent years the simplicity and essential humanity of his poems and songs have touched a ready response everywhere. The emotions which he expressed so vividly and tenderly – love, friendship, tolerance, brotherhood, liberty – are universal, as meaningful to the urban proletariat of Russia and the Chinese peasant as to the higher socio-economic groups in western society.

The first Burns clubs were formed in the early 1800s and undoubtedly relied heavily on personal association with the late poet in their earlier years. Later, clubs were formed in every part of the globe by Scots in exile. The worldwide celebration of his birth centenary and other mammoth demonstrations of popular affection for Burns in the nineteenth century inspired some of the leading Burns enthusiasts of the time to do something more positive about preserving his memory. The Victorians had a penchant for monumental statuary and naturally Burns was the object of a great deal of the statues, memorials and busts erected in the late nineteenth century. In the summer of 1884 a statue of the poet was erected on the Thames Embankment, London and it was while they were walking through the Embankment Gardens at that time that the idea of forming a federation of Burns clubs came to David Mackay (provost of Kilmarnock), Captain David Sneddon and Colin Rae-Brown.

Burnsians from all over the world were due to convene in London the following March for the unveiling of a bust of Burns in Poets' Corner, Westminster Abbey, and in the meantime the idea of a federation took root. A preliminary meeting was held in London in February 1885 at which a draft constitution was formulated and invitations sent out to all the Burns clubs then known to exist. As a result, a meeting of seventeen gentlemen took place in Kilmarnock on 17 July 1885 and the Burns Federation was formally instituted. Progress was very slow at first, but by 1890 some forty-nine clubs in the British Isles, America and Australasia had become affiliated. The following year the Federation launched its annual *Burns Chronicle*. This, more than anything else, stimulated the expansion of the Federation, and the number of clubs which affiliated grew rapidly thereafter.

The primary aim of the Federation was to establish that worldwide and all-embracing brotherhood of man which was the highest ideal of the poet himself, and this has continued to be its main theme. Over the past century more than a thousand Burns clubs and Scottish societies in every part of the world have joined the Federation which today speaks for almost 100,000 Burnsians in a score of countries. Today the Federation includes clubs in every continent, from Manitoba to Mexico, and from Manamah to Melbourne. Moreover, the Federation has played a major role in Burns events all over the world, from the annual conferences staged in Canada and the United States in recent years to the well-attended Burns suppers in Moscow and Peking.

The Constitution of the Federation has been remodelled several times but its main objects have altered little over the years. They are:

1 To encourage the Clubs and Societies who honour Robert Burns
2 To strengthen the bond of fellowship among Burnsians the world over
3 To keep alive the old Scottish tongue
4 To encourage and arrange schoolchildren's competitions, to stimulate the teaching of Scottish history, literature, art and music
5 To mark with suitable inscriptions, repair or renew memorials to Burns and his contemporaries.

Membership is open to all properly constituted Burns clubs and kindred Scottish societies. The headquarters of the Burns Federation is at Kilmarnock, where the movement was founded exactly a century ago. Private individuals can also join the Federation as Associate Members. Over the past hundred years the Federation has played a leading role in the cultural life of Scotland and among its numerous achievements have been the preservation of the Auld Brig o' Ayr from destruction, the institution of the Chair of Scottish History and Literature at Glasgow University and the restoration to Scotland of the priceless Glenriddell Manuscripts. In more recent years the Federation has played a major role in the promotion of the Scottish National Dictionary and the campaign to have a stained-glass window in memory of Burns installed in St Giles Cathedral, Edinburgh. The Federation's school competitions annually attract over 150,000 entries, and it was largely due to the Federation's efforts that Lowland Scots was finally recognised by the Scottish educational authorities as a subject worthy of teaching and study in schools.

James A. Mackay
Editor, Burns Chronicle

My Heart's in the Highlands

The first half-stanza of this song is old.

My heart's in the Highlands, my heart is not here;
My heart's in the Highlands, a-chasing the deer;
A-chasing the wild deer, and following the roe –
My heart's in the Highlands wherever I go.

Farewell to the Highlands, farewell to the North,
The birthplace of valour, the country of worth
Wherever I wander, wherever I rove,
The hills of the Highlands for ever I love.

Farewell to the mountains high cover'd with snow;
Farewell to the straths and green valleys below;
Farewell to the forests and wild-hanging woods;
Farewell to the torrents and loud-pouring floods.

My heart's in the Highlands, my heart is not here;
My heart's in the Highlands a-chasing the deer;
A-chasing the wild deer, and following the roe –
My heart's in the Highlands wherever I go.

Left: the Pass of Killiekrankie, Tayside – once the site of a formidable seventeenth-century battle
Below: the red deer denizen of the high moors and mountains roam in separate herds – females with their young, and the stags. During the rutting season the mountains echo with their eerie calls

Ae Fond Kiss

This is reputed to be the greatest love song ever written.
Dedicated to Nancy McLehose (Clarinda).

Ae fond kiss, and then we sever!
Ae fareweel, and then forever!
Deep in heart-wrung tears I'll pledge thee,
Warring sighs and groans I'll wage thee.

Who shall say that Fortune grieves him,
While the star of hope she leaves him?
Me, nae cheerfu' twinkle lights me,
Dark despair around benights me.

I'll ne'er blame my partial fancy:
Naething could resist my Nancy!
But to see her was to love her,
Love but her, and love for ever.

Had we never lov'd sae kindly,
Had we never lov'd sae blindly,
Never met – or never parted –
We had ne'er been broken-hearted.

Fare-thee-weel, thou first and fairest!
Fare-thee-weel, thou best and dearest!
Thine be ilka joy and treasure,
Peace, Enjoyment, Love and Pleasure!

Ae fond kiss, and then we sever!
Ae fareweel, alas, for ever!
Deep in heart-wrung tears I'll pledge thee,
Warring sighs and groans I'll wage thee.

Ilka – every

The area around Moffat Water, in Dumfries and
Galloway is important for sheep-farming; Moffat was
once an important spa-town and Robert Burns was
among the distinguished visitors who came to take the
waters

A Man's a Man for A' That

Burns said of this song, 'A great critic on songs says that love and wine are the two exclusive schemes for song writing. The following is on neither subject.' Good prose thoughts put into rhyme: a fine song.

Is there, for honest poverty,
   That hangs his head, and a' that?
The coward slave, we pass him by,
   We dare be poor for a' that!
For a' that, and a' that,
   Our toils obscure, and a' that;
The rank is but the guinea-stamp,
   The man's the gowd for a' that!

What though on hamely fare we dine,
   Wear hodden gray, and a' that;
Gie fools their silks, and knaves their wine,
   A man's a man for a' that!
For a' that, and a' that,
   Their tinsel show and a' that;
The honest man, though e'er sae poor,
   Is king o' men for a' that!

Ye see yon birkie, ca'd a lord,
   Wha struts, and stares, and a' that;
Though hundreds worship at his word,
   He's but a coof for a' that:
For a' that, and a' that,
   His riband, star, and a' that;
The man of independent mind,
   He looks and laughs at a' that!

A king can mak a belted knight,
   A marquis, duke, and a' that;
But an honest man's aboon his might.
   Guid faith he maunna fa' that!
For a' that, and a' that,
   Their dignities, and a' that,
The pith o' sense, and pride o' worth,
   Are higher ranks than a' that.

Then let us pray that come it may –
   As come it will for a' that –
That sense and worth, o'er a' the earth,
   May bear the gree, and a' that;
For a' that, and a' that,
   It's comin' yet for a' that,
That man to man, the warld o'er,
   Shall brothers be for a' that!

Birkie – literally the phrase means a mettlesome fellow: here it must be rendered a proud and affected fellow; coof – fool; he maunna fa' that – he must not try that.

Ca' the Ewes

Originally written for the Museum, with a few alterations by Burns.

As I gaed down the water-side,
There I met my shepherd lad,
He row'd me sweetly in his plaid,
  And he ca'd me his dearie.

    Ca' the ewes to the knowes,
    Ca' them whare the heather grows,
    Ca' them whare the burnie rowes,
      My bonny dearie!

Will ye gang down the water-side,
And see the waves sae sweetly glide?
Beneath the hazels spreading wide
  The moon it shines fu' clearly.

I was bred up at nae sic school,
My shepherd lad, to play the fool,
And a' the day to sit in dool,
  And naebody to see me.

Ye sall get gowns and ribbons meet,
Cauf-leather shoon upon your feet,
And in my arms ye'se lie and sleep,
  And ye sall be my dearie.

If ye'll but stand to what ye've said,
I'se gang wi' you, my shepherd lad,
And ye may rowe me in your plaid,
  And I sall be your dearie.

    While waters wimple to the sea;
    While day blinks in the lift sae hie;
    Till clay-cauld death sall blin' my ee,
      Ye sall be my dearie.

Row'd – wrapt; wimple – meander; lift – heavens.

Drumlanrig Castle, Dumfries and Galloway

The wooded banks of Loch Trool, Dumfries and Galloway

The Bonny Wee Thing

Bonny wee thing, cannie wee thing,
   Lovely wee thing, wert thou mine,
I wad wear thee in my bosom,
   Lest my jewel I should tine.
Wishfully I look and languish
   In that bonny face o' thine;
And my heart it stounds wi' anguish,
   Lest my wee thing be na mine.

Wit, and grace, and love, and beauty,
   In ae constellation shine;
To adore thee is my duty,
   Goddess o' this soul o' mine!
Bonny wee thing, cannie wee thing,
   Lovely wee thing, wert thou mine,
I wad wear thee in my bosom,
   Lest my jewel I should tine!

Cannie – gentle; stounds – throbs.

O' Whistle An' I'll Come To Ye My Lad

Chorus
O, whistle an' I'll come to ye, my lad!
O, whistle an' I'll come to ye, my lad!
Tho' father an' mother an' a' should gae mad,
O, whistle an' I'll come to ye, my lad!

But warily tent when ye come to court me,
And come nae unless the back-yett be a-jee;
Syne up the back-style, and let naebody see,
And come as ye were na coming to me,
And come as ye were na coming to me!

At kirk, or at market, whene'er ye meet me,
Gang by me as tho' that ye car'd na a flie;
But steal me a blink o' your bonnie black e'e,
Yet look as ye were na looking to me,
Yet look as ye were na looking to me!

Ay vow and protest that ye care na for me,
And whyles ye may lightly my beauty a wee;
But court nae anither tho' jokin ye be,
For fear that she wyle your fancy frae me,
For fear that she wyle your fancy frae me!

*Gae – go; tent – spy; nae – not; yett – gate; a-jee – ajar; syne – then;
na – not; gang – go; flie – fly; blink o' your bonnie black e'e – glance;
whyles – sometimes; lightly – disparage; wee – little; wyle – entice.*

The charming village of Dean, Edinburgh's New Town, Lothian

Afton Water

*Gilbert Burns affirms he heard his brother say that this song was a
tribute to his dearly loved Highland Mary.*

Flow gently, sweet Afton, among thy green braes,
Flow gently, I'll sing thee a song in thy praise;
My Mary's asleep by thy murmuring stream –
Flow gently, sweet Afton, disturb not her dream.

Thou stock-dove, whose echo resounds through the glen,
Ye wild whistling blackbirds in yon thorny den,
Thou green-crested lapwing, thy screaming forbear –
I charge you disturb not my slumbering fair.

How lofty, sweet Afton, thy neighbouring hills,
Far mark'd with the courses of clear winding rills;
There daily I wander as noon rises high,
My flocks and my Mary's sweet cot in my eye.

How pleasant thy banks and green valleys below,
Where wild in the woodlands the primroses blow;
There, oft as mild evening weeps over the lea,
The sweet-scented birk shades my Mary and me.

Thy crystal stream, Afton, how lovely it glides,
And winds by the cot where my Mary resides;
How wanton thy waters her snowy feet lave,
As gathering sweet flowerets she stems thy clear wave.

Flow gently, sweet Afton, among thy green braes.
Flow gently, sweet river, the theme of my lays;
My Mary's asleep by thy murmuring stream –
Flow gently, sweet Afton, disturb not her dream!

The Bonny Banks of Ayr

The gloomy night is gathering fast,
Loud roars the wild inconstant blast;
Yon murky cloud is foul with rain,
I see it driving o'er the plain;
The hunter now has left the moor,
The scatter'd coveys meet secure;
While here I wander, prest with care
Along the lonely banks of Ayr.

The Autumn mourns her ripening corn,
By early Winter's ravage torn;
Across her placid, azure sky,
She sees the scowling tempest fly:
Chill runs my blood to hear it rave –
I think upon the stormy wave,
Where many a danger I must dare,
Far from the bonny banks of Ayr.

'Tis not the surging billow's roar,
'Tis not that fatal, deadly shore;
Though death in every shape appear,
The wretched have no more to fear!
But round my heart the ties are bound,
That heart transpierced with many a wound;
These bleed afresh, those ties I tear,
To leave the bonny banks of Ayr.

Farewell old Coila's hills and dales,
Her heathy moors and winding vales;
The scenes where wretched fancy roves,
Pursuing past unhappy loves!
Farewell, my friends! farewell, my foes!
My peace with these, my love with those –
The bursting tears my heart declare;
Farewell the bonny banks of Ayr!

Lowland farm near Coulter, Strathclyde. The above song was composed when Burns had made plans to give up farming and emigrate to Jamaica

The Banks o' Doon

Second Version. This song illustrates a genuine experience, the heroine, a lovely and accomplished lady was deserted by her lover after she had borne a son to him.

Ye banks and braes o' bonny Doon,
   How can ye bloom sae fresh and fair;
How can ye chant, ye little birds,
   And I sae weary, fu' o' care!
Thou'll break my heart, thou warbling bird,
   That wantons through the flowering thorn:
Thou minds me o' departed joys,
   Departed – never to return!

Oft hae I roved by bonny Doon,
    To see the rose and woodbine twine;
And ilka bird sang o' its luve,
    And fondly sae did I o' mine.
Wi' lightsome heart I pu'd a rose,
    Fu' sweet upon its thorny tree;
And my fause luver stole my rose,
    But, ah! he left the thorn wi' me.

The famous Burns Monument can be seen in the picture above.
Completed in 1823, this was based on a memorial in Athens. Each
wall faces one of the three traditional Ayrshire regions – Carrick,
Kyle, and Cunninghame. Within the monument are relics of Burns'
time, including a lock of his hair and Highland Mary's bible.

Left and above: the river and Brig o' Doon, Alloway, Strathclyde. This beautiful river is indeed 'bonny' still, with its wooded banks; the bridge was immortalised in *Tam o' Shanter*

Scots, Wha Hae

'There is a tradition', says Burns, in a letter to Thomson, 'that the old air "Hey, Tuttie Taitie" was Robert Bruce's March at the Battle of Bannockburn. This thought in my solitary wanderings, has warmed me to a pitch of enthusiasm; as the theme of liberty and independence which I have thrown into a kind of Scottish ode. Fitted to the air that one might suppose to be the gallant Scots address to his heroic followers on that eventful morning.'

Scots, wha hae wi' Wallace bled,
Scots, wham Bruce has aften led,
Welcome to your gory bed
      Or to victorie!

Now's the day, and now's the hour:
See the front o' battle lour,
See approach proud Edward's power –
      Chains and slaverie!

Wha will be a traitor knave?
Wha can fill a coward's grave?
Wha sae base as be a slave? –
      Let him turn, and flee!

Wha for Scotland's King and Law
Freedom's sword will strongly draw,
Freeman stand or Freeman fa',
      Let him follow me!

By Oppression's woes and pains,
By your sons in servile chains,
We will drain our dearest veins
      But they shall be free!

Lay the proud usurpers low!
Tyrants fall in every foe!
Liberty's in every blow!
      Let us do, or die!

Right: the Bruce Stone is situated at the south-western end of Loch Trool and commemorates Robert Bruce's victory over the English in 1307. This is a beautiful area of oak forestland in Dumfries and Galloway

My Father was a Farmer

*'The following song,' says the poet, 'is a wild rhapsody, miserably
deficient in versification; but the sentiments were the genuine feelings
of my heart at the time it was written.'*

My father was a farmer
   Upon the Carrick border, O,
And carefully he bred me
   In decency and order, O,
He bade me act a manly part,
   Though I had ne'er a farthing, O,
For without an honest manly heart,
   No man was worth regarding, O.

Then out into the world
   My course I did determine, O;
Though to be rich was not my wish,
   Yet to be great was charming, O:
My talents they were not the worst,
   Nor yet my education, O;
Resolved was I at least to try
   To mend my situation, O.

The farm of Mossgiel as it was when lived in by Burns. Engraving by courtesy of Samual K. Gaw

In many a way, and vain essay,
   I courted Fortune's favour, O;
Some cause unseen still stept between,
   To frustrate each endeavour, O:
Sometimes by foes I was o'erpower'd;
   Sometimes by friends forsaken, O;
And when my hope was at the top,
   I still was worst mistaken, O.

Then sore harass'd, and tired at last,
   With Fortune's vain delusion, O,
I dropt my schemes, like idle dreams,
   And came to this conclusion, O:
The past was bad, and the future hid;
   Its good or ill untried, O;
But the present hour was in my power,
   And so I would enjoy it, O.

No help, nor hope, nor view had I,
   Nor person to befriend me, O;
So I must toil, and sweat, and broil,
   And labour to sustain me, O:
To plough and sow, to reap and mow,
   My father bred me early, O;
For one, he said, to labour bred,
   Was a match for Fortune fairly, O.

Thus all obscure, unknown, and poor,
   Through life I'm doom'd to wander, O
Till down my weary bones I lay
   In everlasting slumber, O.
No view nor care, but shun whate'er
   Might breed me pain or sorrow, O;
I live to-day as well's I may,
   Regardless of to-morrow, O.

But cheerful still, I am as well
   As a monarch in a palace, O,
Though Fortune's frown still hunts me down
   With all her wonted malice, O:
I make indeed my daily bread,
   But ne'er can make it farther, O;
But as daily bread is all I need,
   I do not much regard her, O.

When sometimes by my labour
   I earn a little money, O,
Some unforeseen misfortune
   Comes generally upon me, O:
Mischance, mistake, or by neglect,
   Or my good-natured folly, O;
But come what will, I've sworn it still,
   I'll ne'er be melancholy, O.

All you who follow wealth and power
   With unremitting ardour, O,
The more in this you look for bliss,
   You leave your view the farther, O.
Had you the wealth Potosi boasts,
   Or nations to adore you, O,
A cheerful, honest-hearted clown
   I will prefer before you, O!

The Cotter's Saturday Night

*Burns says, 'The cotter, in the Saturday Night, is an exact copy of my
father in his manners, his family devotion, and exhortations; yet the
other parts of the description do not apply to our family.'*

(Selected verses)

My loved, my honour'd, much-respected friend!
  No mercenary Bard his homage pays;
With honest pride, I scorn each selfish end:
  My dearest meed, a friend's esteem and praise:
To you I sing, in simple Scottish lays,
  The lowly train in life's sequester'd scene;
The native feelings strong, the guileless ways:
  What Aiken in a cottage would have been;
Ah! though his worth unknown, far happier there, I ween!

But now the supper crowns their simple board,
  The halesome parritch, chief of Scotia's food:
The soupe their only hawkie does afford,
  That 'yont the hallan snugly chows her cood:
The dame brings forth, in complimental mood,
  To grace the lad, her weel-hain'd kebbuck, fell,
And aft he's prest, and aft he ca's it guid:
  The frugal wifie, garrulous, will tell,
How 'twas a towmond auld, sin' lint was i' the bell.

From scenes like these old Scotia's grandeur springs,
  That makes her loved at home, revered abroad:
Princes and lords are but the breath of kings,
  'An honest man's the noblest work of God;'
And certes, in fair virtue's heavenly road,
  The cottage leaves the palace far behind.
What is a lordling's pomp? – a cumbrous load,
  Disguising oft the wretch of human kind,
Studied in arts of hell, in wickedness refined!

O Scotia! my dear, my native soil!
  For whom my warmest wish to Heaven is sent.
Long may thy hardy sons of rustic toil
  Be blest with health, and peace, and sweet content!
And, oh! may Heaven their simple lives prevent
  From luxury's contagion, weak and vile!
Then, howe'er crown and coronets be rent,
  A virtuous populace may rise the while,
And stand a wall of fire around their much-loved isle.

*Soupe – milk; hawkie – cow; hallan – porch; weel-hain'd kebbuck –
well saved cheese, strong; fell – biting; towmond – twelvemonth.*

View from Murray's Monument by the New Galloway Road, Dumfries and Galloway

O Thou! who pour'd the patriotic tide
    That stream'd through Wallace's undaunted heart,
Who dared to nobly stem tyrannic pride,
    Or nobly die, the second glorious part,
The patriot's God, peculiarly Thou art,
    His friend, inspirer, guardian, and reward!
Oh, never, never, Scotia's realm desert;
    But still the patriot, and the patriot-b'ard,
In bright succession raise, her ornament and guard!

To a Mouse

On turning up her nest with the plough, November 1785.

Wee, sleekit, cowrin', tim'rous beastie,
Oh, what a panic's in thy breastie!
Thou needna start awa' sae hasty,
    Wi' bickering brattle!
I wad be laith to rin and chase thee,
    Wi' murd'ring pattle!

I'm truly sorry man's dominion
Has broken nature's social union,
And justifies that ill opinion
    Which maks thee startle
At me, thy poor earth-born companion,
    And fellow-mortal!

I doubt na, whyles, but thou may thieve;
What then? poor beastie, thou maun live!
A daimen icker in a thrave
    'S a sma' request:
I'll get a blessin' wi' the lave,
    And never miss't!

Thy wee bit housie, too, in ruin!
Its silly wa's the win's are strewin'!
And naething now to big a new ane
    O' foggage green!
And bleak December's winds ensuin',
    Baith snell and keen!

Thou saw the fields laid bare and waste,
And weary winter comin' fast,
And cozie here, beneath the blast,
    Thou thought to dwell,
Till, crash! the cruel coulter past
    Out through thy cell.

That wee bit heap o' leaves and stibble
Has cost thee mony a weary nibble!
Now thou's turn'd out for a' thy trouble,
    But house or hauld,
To thole the winter's sleety dribble,
    And cranreuch cauld!

But, Mousie, thou art no thy lane,
In proving foresight may be vain:
The best-laid schemes o' mice and men
    Gang aft a-gley,
And lea'e us nought but grief and pain
    For promised joy.

Still thou art blest, compared wi' me!
The present only toucheth thee:
But, och! I backward cast me ee
    On prospects drear!
And forward, though I canna see,
    I guess and fear.

Bickering brattle – hurrying run; pattle – plough spade; whyles – sometimes; daimen icker in a thrave – an ear of corn in a thrave, a thrave being twenty-four sheaves; snell – sharp; cozie – comfortable; cranreuch – hoar frost; not thy lane – not alone; gang aft a-gley – go often away.

To commemorate the bi-centenary of the birth of Robert Burns, the Burns Club of London presented a memorial window to the Crown Court Church, Covent Garden. This window was unveiled and dedicated at a service at the church on 24 January 1960. Burns is depicted in the window as a ploughman, ruefully contemplating the destruction of the nest of a field mouse by his plough, holding in his hand the 'Wee, sleekit, cowrin', tim'rous beastie' – the incident which inspired the poem above. The window of stained glass shows the poet in farmer's dress standing against a background of Ayrshire countryside.

Above left: Burns, on turning up a mouse's nest with a plough
Left: Harvest mice, now a rare sight in cornfields

Holy Willie's Prayer

(Selected verses)

O Thou, wha in the heavens dost dwell,
Wha, as it pleases best thysel,
Sends ane to heaven, and ten to hell,
    A' for thy glory,
And no for ony guid or ill
    They've done afore thee!

I bless and praise thy matchless might,
Whan thousands thou hast left in night,
That I am here, afore thy sight,
    For gifts and grace,
A burnin' and a shinin' light
    To a' this place.

What was I, or my generation,
That I should get sic exaltation?
I, wha deserve sic just damnation
    For broken laws,
Five thousand years 'fore my creation,
    Through Adam's cause.

When frae my mither's womb I fell,
Thou might hae plunged me into hell,
To gnash my gums, to weep and wail,
    In burnin' lake,
Whare damned devils roar and yell,
    Chain'd to a stake.

Yet I am here a chosen sample,
To show thy grace is great and ample;
I'm here a pillar in thy temple,
    Strong as a rock,
A guide, a buckler, an example,
    To a' thy flock.

O Lord, thou kens what zeal I bear,
When drinkers drink, and swearers swear,
And singing there, and dancing here,
    Wi' great and sma';
For I am keepit, by thy fear,
    Free frae them a'.

But yet, O Lord! confess I must,
At times I'm fash'd wi' fleshly lust;
And sometimes, too, wi' warldly trust,
    Vile self gets in;
But thou remembers we are dust,
    Defiled in sin.

Dunure, near Ayr, Strathclyde

O Lord! yestreen, thou kens, wi' Meg –
Thy pardon I sincerely beg,
Oh, may it ne'er be a livin' plague,
        To my dishonour,
And I'll ne'er lift a lawless leg
        Again upon her.

Besides, I farther maun avow,
Wi' Lizzie's lass, three times I trow –
But, Lord, that Friday I was fou'
        When I came near her,
Or else, thou kens, thy servant true
        Wad ne'er hae steer'd her.

Maybe thou lets this fleshly thorn
Beset thy servant e'en and morn,
Lest he owre high and proud should turn,
        'Cause he's sae gifted;
If sae, thy han' maun e'en be borne
        Until thou lift it.

Lord, bless thy chosen in this place,
For here thou hast a chosen race:
But God confound their stubborn face,
        And blast their name,
Wha bring thy elders to disgrace
        And public shame.

Lord, mind Gawn Hamilton's deserts,
He drinks, and swears, and plays at cartes,
Yet has sae mony takin' arts,
        Wi' grit and sma',
Frae God's ain priests the people's hearts
        He steals awa'.

And when we chasten'd him therefore,
Thou kens how he bred sic a splore,
As set the world in a roar
        O' laughin' at us; –
Curse thou his basket and his store,
        Kail and potatoes.

Lord, hear my earnest cry and prayer
Against the presbyt'ry of Ayr;
Thy strong right hand, Lord, mak it bare
        Upo' their heads,
Lord, weigh it down, and dinna spare,
        For their misdeads.

Fash'd – troubled; splore – disturbance.

Looking towards the 822-foot-high Arthur's Seat, at Edinburgh

The River Tay near Dunkeld, Tayside

Epitaph on Holy Willie

Here Holy Willie's sair worn clay
    Taks up its last abode;
His saul has ta'en some other way,
    I fear the left-hand road.

Stop! there he is, as sure's a gun,
    Poor silly body, see him;
Nae wonder he's as black's the grun,
    Observe wha's standing wi' him!

Your brunstane devilship, I see,
    Has got him there before ye;
But haud your nine-tail cat a wee,
    Till ance ye've heard my story.

Your pity I will not implore,
    For pity ye hae nane!
Justice, alas! has gien him o'er,
    And mercy's day is gane.

But hear me, sir, deil as ye are,
    Look something to your credit;
A coof like him wad stain your name,
    If it were kent ye did it.

Epistle to Davie, A Brother Poet

While winds frae aff Ben Lomond blaw,
And bar the doors wi' driving snaw,
    And hing as owre the ingle,
I set me down to pass the time,
And spin a verse or twa o' rhyme,
    In hamely westlin jingle.
While frosty winds blaw in the drift,
    Ben to the chimla lug,
I grudge a wee the great folk's gift,
That lives sae bien and snug:
        I tent less, and want less
            Their roomy fire-side;
        But hanker and canker
            To see their cursèd pride.

It's hardly in a body's power
To keep at times frae being sour,
    To see how things are shared;
How best o' chiels are whiles in want,
While coofs on countless thousands rant,
    And ken na how to wear't;
But Davie, lad, ne'er fash your head,
    Though we hae little gear,
We're fit to win our daily bread,
    As lang's we're hale and fier:
        'Mair spier na, nor fear na,'
            Auld age ne're mind a feg,
        The last o't, the warst o't,
            Is only but to beg.

It's no in titles nor in rank:
It's no in wealth like Lon'on bank,
    To purchase peace and rest:
It's no in making muckle mair;
It's no in books; it's no in lear;
    To make us truly blest;
If happiness hae not her seat
    And centre in the breast,
We may be wise, or rich, or great,
    But never can be blest:
        Nae treasures, nor pleasures,
            Could make us happy lang:
        The heart aye's the part aye
            That makes us right or wrang.

*Hing us owre the ingle – double us up over the fire; jingle – homely
west country dialect; lug – chimney corner; bien – comfortable; tent –
head; chiels – fellows; coofs – fools; fash – trouble; gear – goods or
wealth; fier – whole and sound; mair spier – more ask; feg – fig;
muckle mair – much more.*

Ben Lomond is the highest mountain overlooking Loch Lomond, seen here in autumn

Address to Edinburgh

Burns, when writing to his friend William Chalmers, sent him the
following poem.

Edina! Scotia's darling seat!
  All hail thy palaces and towers,
Where once beneath a monarch's feet
  Sat Legislation's sovereign powers!
From marking wildly-scatter'd flowers,
  As on the banks of Ayr I stray'd,
And singing, lone, the lingering hours,
  I shelter in thy honour'd shade.

Here wealth still swells the golden tide,
  As busy Trade his labour plies;
There Architecture's noble pride
  Bids elegance and splendour rise;
Here Justice, from her native skies,
  High wields her balance and her rod;
There Learning, with his eagle eyes,
  Seeks Science in her coy abode.

Thy sons, Edina! social, kind,
  With open arms the stranger hail;
Their views enlarged, their liberal mind,
  Above the narrow, rural vale;
Attentive still to Sorrow's wail,
  Or modest Merit's silent claim;
And never may their sources fail!
  And never envy blot their name!

Thy daughters bright thy walks adorn,
  Gay as the gilded summer sky,
Sweet as the dewy milk-white thorn,
  Dear as the raptured thrill of joy!
Fair Burnet strikes th' adoring eye,
  Heaven's beauties on my fancy shine;
I see the Sire of Love on high,
  And own His work indeed divine.

There, watching high the least alarms,
  Thy rough, rude fortress gleams afar;
Like some bold veteran, gray in arms,
  And mark'd with many a seamy scar:
The ponderous wall and massy bar,
  Grim-rising o'er the rugged rock,
Have oft withstood assailing war,
  And oft repell'd the invader's shock.

With awe-struck thought, and pitying tears,
  I view that noble, stately dome,
Where Scotia's kings of other years,
  Famed heroes! had their royal home;
Alas, how changed the times to come!
  Their royal name low in the dust!
Their hapless race wild-wandering roam!
  Though rigid law cries out, 'Twas just.

Wild beats my heart to trace your steps,
  Whose ancestors, in days of yore,
Through hostile ranks and ruin'd gaps
  Old Scotia's bloody lion bore:
Even I who sing in rustic lore,
  Haply, my sires have left their shed,
And faced grim Danger's loudest roar,
  Bold-following where your fathers led!

Edina! Scotia's darling seat!
  All hail thy palaces and towers,
Where once beneath a monarch's feet
  Sat Legislation's sovereign powers!
From marking wildly-scatter'd flowers,
  As on the banks of Ayr I stray'd,
And singing, lone, the lingering hours,
  I shelter in thy honour'd shade.

Edinburgh Castle from King's Stables.
Painting by Mrs J. Stewart Smith; by courtesy of the Central Library, Edinburgh

The Highland Laddie

*An improvement and expansion of: 'The Highland Lad and the
Lowland Lassie'.*

The bonniest lad that e'er I saw,
    Bonny laddie, Highland laddie,
Wore a plaid, and was fu' braw,
    Bonny Highland laddie.
On his head a bonnet blue,
    Bonny laddie, Highland laddie;
His royal heart was firm and true,
    Bonny Highland laddie.

Trumpets sound, and cannons roar,
    Bonny lassie, Lowland lassie;
And a' the hills wi' echoes roar,
    Bonny Lowland lassie.
Glory, honour, now invite,
    Bonny lassie, Lowland lassie,
For freedom and my king to fight,
    Bonny Lowland lassie.

The sun a backward course shall take,
    Bonny laddie, Highland laddie,
Ere aught thy manly courage shake,
    Bonny Highland laddie.
Go! for yoursel procure renown,
    Bonny laddie, Highland laddie;
And for your lawful king his crown,
    Bonny Highland laddie.

Bonny Highland Laddies; by courtesy of the Edinburgh City Police Pipe Band

Burns Cottage, Alloway. In the right-hand corner of the picture is the bed in which Burns was born

Verses to my Bed

Thou bed, in which I first began
To be that various creature – man!
And when again the fates decree,
The place where I must cease to be; –
When sickness comes, to whom I fly,
To soothe my pain, or close mine eye; –
When cares surround me where I weep,
Or lose them all in balmy sleep; –
When sore with labour, whom I court,
And to thy downy breast resort –
Where, too, ecstatic joys I find,
When deigns my Delia to be kind –
And full of love, in all her charms,
Thou givest the fair one to my arms,
The centre thou, where grief and pain,
Disease and rest, alternate reign.
Oh, since within thy little space
So many various scenes take place;
Lessons as useful shalt thou teach
As sages dictate – churchmen preach;
And man, convinced by thee alone,
This great important truth shall own: –
That thin partitions do divide
The bounds where good and ill reside;
That nought is perfect here below;
But bliss still bordering upon woe.

Tam o' Shanter

(Selected verses)

When chapman billies leave the street,
And drouthy neibors neibors meet,
As market days are wearin' late,
And folk begin to tak the gate;
While we sit bousing at the nappy,
And gettin' fou and unco happy,
We think na on the lang Scots miles,
The mosses, waters, slaps, and stiles,
That lie between us and our hame,
Wh'are sits our sulky sullen dame,
Gathering her brows like gathering storm,
Nursing her wrath to keep it warm.

This truth fand honest Tam o' Shanter,
As he frae Ayr ae night did canter,
(Auld Ayr, wham ne'er a town surpasses
For honest men and bonny lasses).

But to our tale: – Ae market night,
Tam had got planted unco right,
Fast by an ingle, bleezing finely,
Wi' reaming swats, that drank divinely;
And at his elbow, Souter Johnny,
His ancient, trusty, drouthy crony;
Tam lo'ed him like a vera brither –
They had been fou for weeks thegither!
The night drave on wi' sangs and clatter,
And aye the ale was growing better:
The landlady and Tam grew gracious,
Wi' favours secret, sweet, and precious;
The Souter tauld his queerest stories,
The landlord's laugh was ready chorus:
The storm without might rair and rustle –
Tam didna mind the storm a whistle.

Care, mad to see a man sae happy,
E'en drown'd himsel amang the nappy!
As bees flee hame wi' lades o' treasure,
The minutes wing'd their way wi' pleasure:
Kings may be blest, but Tam was glorious,
O'er a' the ills o' life victorious!

But pleasures are like poppies spread,
You seize the flower, its bloom is shed!
Or like the snowfall in the river,
A moment white – then melts for ever;
Or like the borealis race,
That flit ere you can point their place;
Or like the rainbow's lovely form,
Evanishing amid the storm.
Nae man can tether time or tide;
The hour approaches Tam maun ride;
That hour, o' night's black arch the keystane,
That dreary hour he mounts his beast in;
And sic a night he taks the road in
As ne'er poor sinner was abroad in.

The wind blew as 'twad blawn its last;
The rattling showers rose on the blast;
The speedy gleams the darkness swallow'd;
Loud, deep, and lang, the thunder bellow'd:
That night, a child might understand
The deil had business on his hand.

Weel mounted on his gray mare, Meg,
A better never lifted leg,
Tam skelpit on through dub and mire,
Despising wind, and rain, and fire;
Whiles holding fast his guid blue bonnet,
Whiles crooning o'er some auld Scots sonnet;
Whiles glowering round wi' prudent cares,
Lest bogles catch him unawares:
Kirk-Alloway was drawing nigh,
Whare ghaists and houlets nightly cry.

Ah, Tam! ah, Tam! thou'lt get thy fairin'!
In hell they'll roast thee like a herrin'!
In vain thy Kate awaits thy comin'!
Kate soon will be a woefu' woman!
Now, do thy speedy utmost, Meg,
And win the keystane of the brig;
There at them thou thy tail may toss,
A running stream they darena cross;

*Billies – fellows; drouthy – thirsty; gate – road; nappy – ale; unco –
unusually; ingle – fire; reaming swats – foaming ale; rair – roar;
skelpit – rode with careless speed; crooning – humming; glowering –
peering; bogles – spirits; fairin' – deserts; fient – never; ettle – design.*

Tam o' Shanter by James Drummond; by courtesy of the Trustees of Burns Cottage and Monument, Alloway

But ere the keystane she could make,
The fient a tail she had to shake!
For Nannie, far before the rest,
Hard upon noble Maggie prest,
And flew at Tam wi' furious ettle;
But little wist she Maggie's mettle –
Ae spring brought off her master hale,
But left behind her ain gray tail:
The carlin caught her by the rump,
Aud left poor Maggie scarce a stump.

Now, wha this tale o' truth shall read,
Ilk man and mother's son, take heed:
Whane'er to drink you are inclined,
Or cutty-sarks run in your mind,
Think! ye may buy the joys owre dear –
Remember Tam o' Shanter's mare.

Charlie He's My Darling

Chorus
An' Charlie he's my darling,
My darling, my darling,
Charlie he's my darling –
    The Young Chevalier!

'Twas on a Monday morning
   Right early in the year,
That Charlie came to our town –
   The Young Chevalier!

As he was walking up the street
   The city for to view,
O, there he spied a bonie lass
   The window looking thro'!

Sae light's he jimped up the stair,
   And tirl'd at the pin;
And wha sae ready as hersel'
   To let the laddie in!

He set his Jenny on his knee,
   All in his Highland dress;
For brawlie weel he kend the way
   To please a bonie lass.

It's up yon heathery mountain
   And down yon scroggy glen,
We daurna gang a-milking
   For Charlie and his men!

Tirl'd – rasped; brawlie weel – finely well; scroggy – scrubby; daurna
gang – daren't go.

Prince Charles Edward Stuart. On his right stands Lochiel, Chief of Clan Cameron. On his left, Pitsligo, Chief of the Clan Forbes. From the painting by Pettie. By Gracious Permission of Her Majesty the Queen. This painting currently hangs in the Inner State Room at the Palace of Holyrood house.

A Red, Red Rose

An improvement of a street ballad.

Oh, my luve's like a red, red rose,
That's newly sprung in June:
Oh, my luve's like the melodie
That's sweetly play'd in tune.

As fair art thou, my bonny lass,
So deep in luve am I;
And I will luve thee still, my dear,
Till a' the seas gang dry.

Till a' the seas gang dry, my dear,
And the rocks melt wi' the sun:
I will luve thee still, my dear,
While the sands o' life shall run.

And fare thee weel, my only luve!
And fare thee weel a while!
And I will come again, my luve,
Though it were ten thousand mile.

The attractive red blooming rose 'Allen Chandler'

Loch Eck, Strathclyde

My Wife's a Winsome Wee Thing

She is a winsome wee thing,
She is a handsome wee thing,
She is a bonny wee thing,
　This sweet wee wife o' mine.

I never saw a fairer,
I never lo'ed a dearer;
And neist my heart I'll wear her,
　For fear my jewel tine.

She is a winsome wee thing,
She is a handsome wee thing,
She is a bonny wee thing,
　This sweet wee wife o' mine.

The warld's wrack we share o't,
The warstle and the care o't;
Wi' her I'll blithely bear it,
　And think my lot divine.

Tine – be lost.

Highland Mary

Ye banks, and braes, and streams around
  The castle o' Montgomery,
Green be your woods, and fair your flowers,
  Your waters never drumlie!
There simmer first unfauld her robes,
  And there the langest tarry;
For there I took the last fareweel
  O' my sweet Highland Mary.

How sweetly bloom'd the gay green birk!
  How rich the hawthorn's blossom!
As underneath their fragrant shade,
  I clasp'd her to my bosom!
The golden hours, on angel wings,
  Flew o'er me and my dearie;
For dear to me, as light and life,
  Was my sweet Highland Mary!

Wi' mony a vow, and lock'd embrace,
  Our parting was fu' tender;
And, pledging aft to meet again,
  We tore oursels asunder;
But, oh! fell Death's untimely frost,
  That nipt my flower sae early! –
Now green's the sod, and cauld's the clay,
  That wraps my Highland Mary!

Oh, pale, pale now, those rosy lips,
  I aft hae kiss'd sae fondly!
And closed for aye the sparkling glance
  That dwelt on me sae kindly!
And mouldering now in silent dust
  That heart that lo'ed me dearly –
But still within my bosom's core
  Shall live my Highland Mary!

Mary Campbell was born at Auchamore Farm in Dunoon, Argyll. A statue to her memory stands out on Castle Hill – looking towards the Ayrshire coast.

Below: an engraving of Coilsfield House, the mansion of Colonel Hugh Montgomery. This is the place Burns called 'The castle o' Montgomery' in the poem above. Mary Campbell was employed here as a dairymaid. The engraving shows the finest part of the domain on the immediate banks of the Faile, where, in all probability, the last farewell of Burns and his Highland Mary took place. From *The Land of Burns Division 2*, written by Professor Wilson and Robert Chambers. By courtesy of Mr T. McIlwraith

Sunset over Loch Shiel, Highland

To Mary in Heaven

Thou ling'ring star, with less'ning ray,
　　That lovest to greet the early morn,
Again thou usher'st in the day
　　My Mary from my soul was torn.
O Mary! dear departed shade!
　　Where is thy place of blissful rest?
See'st thou thy lover lowly laid?
　　Hear'st thou the groans that rend his breast?

That sacred hour can I forget,
　　Can I forget the hallow'd grove,
Where by the winding Ayr we met,
　　To live one day of parting love!
Eternity will not efface
　　Those records déar of transports past;
Thy image at our last embrace;
　　Ah! little thought we 'twas our last!

Ayr, gurgling, kiss'd his pebbled shore,
　　O'erhung with wild woods, thick'ning green;
The fragrant birch, and hawthorn hoar,
　　Twined amorous round the raptured scene;
The flowers sprang wanton to be prest,
　　The birds sang love on every spray –
Till too, too soon, the glowing west
　　Proclaim'd the speed of wingèd day.

Still o'er these scenes my memory wakes,
　　And fondly broods with miser care!
Time but the impression stronger makes,
　　As streams their channels deeper wear.
My Mary! dear departed shade!
　　Where is thy place of blissful rest?
See'st thou thy lover lowly laid?
　　Hear'st thou the groans that rend his breast?

The Farewell

*'The following touching stanzas,' says Cunningham, 'were composed
in the autumn of 1786, when the prospects of the poet darkened, and
he looked towards the West Indies as a place of refuge, and perhaps of
hope. All who shared his affections are mentioned – but in nothing he
ever wrote was his affection for Jean Armour more tenderly or more
naturally displayed.'*

Farewell, old Scotia's bleak domains,
Far dearer than the torrid plains
  Where rich ananas blow!
Farewell, a mother's blessing dear!
A brother's sigh! a sister's tear!
  My Jean's heart-rending throe!
Farewell, my Bess! though thou'rt bereft
  Of my parental care;
A faithful brother I have left,
  My part in him thou'lt share!
    Adieu too, to you too,
      My Smith, my bosom frien';
    When kindly you mind me,
      Oh, then befriend my Jean!

What bursting anguish tears my heart!
From thee, my Jeanie, must I part!
  Thou, weeping, answerest, 'No!'
Alas! misfortune stares my face,
And points to ruin and disgrace,
  I, for thy sake, must go!
Thee, Hamilton and Aiken dear,
  A grateful, warm, adieu!
I, with a much-indebted tear,
  Shall still remember you!
    All hail then, the gale then,
      Wafts me from thee, dear shore!
    It rustles and whistles –
      I'll never see thee more!

Dumfries, Dumfries and Galloway

The Deil's awa' wi' th' Exciseman

The deil cam fiddling through the town,
    And danced awa' wi' the Exciseman,
And ilka wife cries – 'Auld Mahoun,
    I wish you luck o' the prize, man!'

The deil's awa', the deil's awa',
    The deil's awa' wi' the Exciseman;
He's danced awa', he's danced awa',
    He's danced awa' wi' the Exciseman!

We'll mak our maut, we'll brew our drink,
    We'll dance, and sing, and rejoice, man;
And mony braw thanks to the meikle black deil
    That danced awa' wi' the Exciseman.

The deil's awa', the deil's awa',
    The deil's awa' wi' the Exciseman;
He's danced awa', he's danced awa',
    He's danced awa' wi' the Exciseman!

There's threesome reels, there's foursome reels,
    There's hornpipes and strathspeys, man;
But the ae best dance e'er cam to the land,
    Was – the deil's awa' wi' the Exciseman.

The deil's awa', the deil's awa',
    The deil's awa' wi' the Exciseman;
He's danced awa', he's danced awa',
    He's danced awa' wi' the Exciseman!

Left: a model of Burns dressed as an Exciseman, by courtesy of Nithsdale District Council. **Right:** chalk drawing of Burns by Archibald Scriving, by courtesy of the National Galleries of Scotland, Edinburgh

The River Clyde at Rosebank, Strathclyde

For the Sake o' Somebody

My heart is sair – I dare na tell –
My heart is sair for Somebody;
I could wake a winter night
For the sake o' Somebody.
Oh-hon! for Somebody!
Oh-hey! for Somebody!
I could range the world around,
For the sake o' Somebody!

Ye Powers that smile on virtuous love,
Oh, sweetly smile on Somebody!
Frae ilka danger keep him free,
And send me safe my Somebody.
Oh-hon! for Somebody!
Oh-hey! for Somebody!
I wad do – what wad I not?
For the sake o' Somebody!

Burns' 'Thank you' to Robert Aiken

From the *Burns Chronicle*

When he and she, baith young and auld,
  Were bent on my undoin'
And tried by lees and scandal bauld
  To drive me clean to ruin.
Wha never aince withdrew his smile,
  Or listened to the claiken?
Ah, he's a frien' that's worth the while,
  A man like Robert Aiken!

When I tried my rustic pen
  In little bits o' rhymin',
Wha introduced me but and ben
  And helped me in my climbin'?
Wha advertised abroad my name,
  'A minstrel in the makin','
Wha fairly read me into fame,
  But lawyer Robert Aiken!

And when wi' muckle qualms I socht
  To get my poems printed,
While mony 'frien's' nae copies bocht
  And some their orders stinted,
Wha by the dizzen and the score
  The names to me was rakin'?
The king o' a' the buying corps
  Was surely Robert Aiken!

The time will come when I'll be deemed
  A poet, grander, greater,
Than ever prophesied or dreamed,
  The loodest, proodest prater.
Then let this fact be published too
  That at the bard's awakin'
The truest, kindest friend he knew
  Was honest Robert Aiken!

Bust of Robert Burns in Poets' Corner, Westminster Abbey

Auld Lang Syne

*Burns first sent this famous song to his friend Mrs Dunlop on
17 December 1788; he wrote, 'Is not the phrase "Auld Lang Syne"
exceedingly impressive', and when he eventually sent it to Thomson of
Dumfries he finished his letter with, 'one more song and I am done,
"Auld Lang Syne".'*

Should auld acquaintance be forgot,
   And never brought to min'?
Should auld acquaintance be forgot,
   And days o' lang syne?

For auld lang syne, my dear:
   For auld lang syne,
We'll tak a cup o' kindness yet
   For auld lang syne!

We twa hae run about the braes,
   And pu'd the gowans fine;
But we've wander'd mony a weary foot
   Sin' auld lang syne.

We twa hae paidl't i' the burn,
   Frae morning sun till dine:
But seas between us braid hae roar'd
   Sin' auld lang syne.

And here's a hand, my trusty fiere,
   And gies a hand o' thine;
And we'll tak a right guid willie-waught
   For auld lang syne!

And surely ye'll be your pint-stoup,
   And surely I'll be mine;
And we'll tak a cup o' kindness yet,
   For auld lang syne.

Auld lang syne – old long ago; fiere – friend; willie-waught – draught.

Above: engraving of Burns at Roslin, by Alexander Nasmyth.
By courtesy of the National Galleries of Scotland, Edinburgh

Front cover: Robert Burns seeking the hand of Mary Campbell (Highland Mary) at Failford;
by courtesy of the Trustees of Burns Cottage and Monument, Alloway

Back cover: full-length portrait of Robert Burns by Alexander Nasmyth;
by courtesy of the National Galleries of Scotland, Edinburgh

Acknowledgements
I would like to thank all those who have generously given their help and advice during the preparation of this
book. To John Manson, Curator of the Burns Cottage Museum, for his inspiration and help in the initial
stages; to Tom McIlwraith, past President of the Burns Federation, for his untiring assistance; to David
Lockwood, Curator of the Dumfries Museums, for his kindness and encouragement; and to James Mackay,
Editor of the *Burns Chronicle*, for his support. Thanks are also due to Sam Gaw, past President of the Burns
Federation; the Irvine Burns Club; the Irvine Development Corporation; the City of Edinburgh; and the
Central Library, Edinburgh. I am also especially grateful to Mrs Maxwell-Scot; the National Galleries of
Scotland; the National Trust for Scotland; and, of course, to Jarrold Colour Publications for transforming my
original idea into this book.

ISBN 0–7117–0194–6 hard covers
ISBN 0–7117–0187–3 paperback